the blue gab

a collection of poetry and prose

by Lydia Redwine

To Ciera,

Here is to become strong
in your weakness,

Lydi

the blue gabled house

a collection of poetry and prose

by Lydia Redwine

Other books by
Lydia Redwine:

Eva Goes Swimming For Hope

Instruments of Sacrifice:
Spirit Followers
Keepers of the Crown

Essence of An Age:
A Collection of Poetry and Prose

To my mother,
my best teacher

contents:

"That is why, for Christ's sake, I delight in weaknesses, in insults, in hardships, in persecutions, in difficulties. For when I am weak, then I am strong."

2 Corinthians 12:10

001. *pretty boys, party girls*

A chaotic balance of concussion and adrenaline,
near transcendent blend of the divine:
a demon's medicinal drink, an angel's liar.
The reaching of a vagrant to immortal grounds
 - *a prayer.*

These immortal grounds speak,
"Wear your crowns,
O knights deemed weak
and damsels bleak!"

Princes and paupers can both be pretty,
princesses and prudes can both be bitchy,
as though "pretty" and "bitchy" are the only
appellations we apply as accolades,
to sort the red plastic cups
from the glass bottles rimmed in cherry-red
chapstick.

Party girls are diamond chokers,
shots of glitter by the smoke-stained windows,
diaries burned at the corners.

"The maidens have gone mad,"
                        they sing.
"Better to be heartless than naive,"
                        the party girl sings.

She sings:
"He is made of gold,
of italics and bold.
He is pretty boy,
he is shiny new toy.
The girls wear flowers
and the boys play games,
so why do I throw their names
like they're darts
and he's a bullseye?
I'm aiming,
won't miss,
cuz' he's pretty boy,
he's bubblegum kiss,
minty mist.
He's butterfly king,
VHS Lord,
Puck of my midsummer dream."

And the party girls are the faeries
who once roamed these forest mounds,
these veiled, sacred grounds
before red ink crossed them out at the thighs,
filled their wombs with vinegar lies,
and idle dreams of pretty boys playing kings.

But of course, it is all for play...
until the party becomes a gun,
a showdown borne of seasons of oppression.

A blessed trauma it is then
to dwell on the outside -
to leave this pity party, bloodbath beginning
behind...
behind in a haze of dreams shattered beneath the
table.

Glass in our palms,
bullets in our throats.

The sirens scream,
but we are silent,

fallen

n

o

t

e

s.

002. my best friend as a lost summer

The radio stutters along to a song we sing of summers we've forgotten.

This August heat we breathe, thighs sticking to cherry-red car seats, our sweat as diamonds because this getaway is our stage.

I sent you a message last November about what this last summer childhood would lend before you went to college.

Where you and I and our friends would Fourth of July weekend spend at your grandparents' cabin.

And I'd collect the cards strayed from their deck and the red plastic cups with our names on them as souvenirs.

This summer's catastrophes are birthed of idle minds, stillborn dreams, dried wishing wells and famined romantical regimes.

In this three month prison disguised as heaven's waiting room, our voices echo an anthem: trauma and split ends.
Dead ends. Beginnings of ends.

At odds with these ends we shall ever be.

For "once upon a time" feels far away, and "happily ever after" is at the bottom of the coke and vodka.

"Prince Charming" is a prom king, slipping a maidenhead over his finger as a ring.
The girls are dragons, the roofs at dusk are their castles.

Forever an intruding guest is this doom, like mother nature lamenting my empty womb.

Violent is the kindness of my friend who will hand me a cracked mirror and hold me despite the blood lingering beneath my nails.

We talk about boys like they're glow sticks, I like them in the pool, and you like them on your neck.

We are companions found in suburban legends, kindred spirits in a time capsule, the best mixtape ever made.

It was an accident of course.
Like almost everything is with us.

Our dormant days coalesced into volcanic weekends, zenithed into simmering sundays where somnolent interchanges were chalked into the concrete.

There is no world without verona walls just as there is no world without rules to break, rebellions to be ignited in the front seat of his car, with the stripes of innocence's leave's whip.

But the sting is sweet, because you are my coral colored baths, the glitter in the sink from last night's hoodwink.

You are paper stars on my ceiling, sleeping on Saturn's rings.
You are a friend I love. I love you, friend. To the very end of this summer

and back again.

003. the ache of august

On front porches and simmering sidewalks,
my best friend and I talk about tattoos.
Her mother won't let her get one,
but she's eighteen now and in college
and far from home
and she has a steady babysitting gig
that will help her pay for one.
I ask her what she will get,
and it is different every time.
Mostly its mountains
or a piece of a home she has yet to find.
Home moves and she moves,
she hates goodbyes and hellos
to people she knows
she will one day say goodbye too.
Mostly, it is something that will remind her
that she can go look for her birth mother
if she wants to.
But she doesn't have to
if she doesn't want to.
We sit on a roof and eat ice cream.
This is the ache of august,
where I remember all the boys I thought
I had loved who were born in this
sacred, simmering month
and she remembers that home can be this:
a friend and a whisper,
songs and ice cream and memory.
"What will *you* get?" she asks.

"To whatever end," encircling my wrist.
I will love her, to whatever end.

004. the princes ride their white stallions
through the supermarket

and we all turn to stare
at their god-like chiseled jawlines and golden hair.
We find it obtrusive yet cathartic.

It really isn't fair,
how when they smash the produce
on the floor that the janitor had mopped overnight,

that

no

one

stops them.

Because they are princes
and they ride white horses.
Princes are *good*,
and so are the riders of white horses.
Haven't you seen the movies
and read the Westerns?

So while they can vaunt of a life without care,
all we know is to stare
and write them into songs,
and carve their names into
our bed-frames and our palms.

There will be no rescind,
no revoke or cancelation.
Their cajoling begins with
offering milk cartons to the
house-wives and carrying
the fragile cases of eggs to the car.

It's stealing a pack of gum in the supermarket this
morning
and her maiden-head in the back parking-lot
tonight.

005. a rebel in his youth

A rebel in his youth is just as poetic
as the death of the most beautiful maiden,
because without the rebellion there is no poem,
and without youth there is no one
who bears these metaphors like blades in his chest
in the next century over.

006. *a maiden in her maddening*

The pick-up truck on the road
rattles rust-ridden to the abode
of a girl who has bent her knees
into blackberry patches
and cricket-buzzed grasses
to lift her head and pray.

It passes the bridge where the slashes
of damnation have been smothered with
shards of sunlight and yellow spray paint.
There are halos and daisies now, but
somehow, *that isn't enough.*

She tells her mother in the morning
that God told her to go to war,
that the taste of blood and salt and
warning, she knows better than most
people.

And her mother punches the dough
with the same knuckles that have painted
Joan's cheek royal - crimson and purple.
"That's nice, sweetie.
I just wish you weren't crazy,
like your father."

Her father grows tomatoes,
and it is in his garden that she meets
them:
Michael
& Margaret
& Catherine.

They have told her to burn her gingham
skirts and to stitch roses into her jeans.
They tell her how to use poems as guns
and words as bullets towards monsters in
pulpits, songs as bandaids,
and hymns as stained-glass blades.
They show her how to tighten her belt
so fumbling fingers can't find how to
unfasten in dark ally-ways and
dusk-stained fields.

So when she runs into the dusty
twilight from the men who scream
"whore,"
and "woman,"
and "devil,"
she finds the back-door shut,
the front door locked,
the windows fastened and the
rusted-truck gone.

There is no home,
no mother,
no father,
no friend.

Just a vast empty sky,
a hundred days, and the
angels with their arms open wide.

So at nineteen, she is burned on a bridge
and thrown into the river.
This is war:
being what you were made to be.

007. july

So, now it seems,
we are okay with these silent streets
as opposed to vodka
and vinegar-bathed sheets.
The colors of a bruised,
lilac sky are somehow
more radiant than the
kaleidoscopes of our minds
when we are high.
High off false expectations
that we will flee this prison
they call youth.

008. the fume of sighs

This is Summer aching and swollen
like a woman before she is a mother cloven.

This is Summer half asleep,
on her belly in briars deep,
harvest moons in her palms,
cricket-buzzed are her songs.

This is Summer splintering from forever,
telling you as you traverse
these fair grounds that this is over,
over when the last apple is plucked,
and the caramel on our lacquered lips
sucked.

The ferris wheel groans
(it is an old man)
The children laugh
(they should while they can.)

This is the end of Summer
and the fume of sighs,
when our backburner dreams come alive,

come alive

and burn

and

burn

and

burn.

We sigh in the streets, under the lights,
by the popcorn stands in our ill-timed feats.
This night isn't sweet.
The cotton candy tastes like dust.
There are no more butterflies on the rides anymore.

There is only the long drive home.

009. we take shots from the fountain of youth

This town has played at this ruse
since our parents were 13 and full of refuse.
The calamine colored sky screams
anthems of infection and tarnished dreams.

"What is the ruse?" you ask.
That we can grow up
and leave
and stay all at once.

This is swallowing a bitter medicinal drink:
when we are told we must leave
and never return to the womb,
never spare a second glance at our old rooms.

All of this is poetry.
Growing up is poetry.
Summertime is poetry.
Sitting on the porch at dusk
and cleaving the concepts of
adulthood into smaller pieces
to eat like glass is poetry.

It is a cage, this poetry,
this pursuit of everything.

They want *everything* for us:
a good education,
a good job,
a good house,
a good family.

But what is good but what we already know?

They tell us to go study business,
or accounting
or the body
or the Law.

But I'd rather study the floor,
the bend of the trees,
the bruises in the last apple,
the bruises on my own body.
How did I get them?
How do I love them?

We are taught about the plasma membrane
but not how to cry in a crowded room
and be okay with that.

So, we hide in our rooms,
our cars parked in fields,
behind the bleachers,
and we take shots from the fountain of youth.

010. *after tylbalt's death*

Romeo and Juliet sit across from each other in a
cherry-red booth;
one milkshake, two straws, and a basket of fries
between them.
Somewhere between the midwest corn fields and
the border of California,
there is a rundown gas station and a diner where
they remember
just how far they have run and that Verona
(small town home)
is not something you run from but something you
carry with you.
If you kill someone in the back alley of your
hometown,
you might just kill someone else at the remote gas
station in New Mexico and go to a diner after.
There will be blood in the trunk of your car and
later on in your sheets in the motel.
But what matters is that you got away, that you did
not, in the end, stay.
The tragedy is not that they both die at the end, it is
that, first, they got away.

011. can you hear the violence?

Can you hear the violence in the streets?
Tybalt has been struck
and this is how death greets
the youth of Midwest America and every place
we find for secrets to keep.

We'd rather count suicides than stars,
(Ophelia and Othello,
Brutus and Cassius
and how many more?)
and cuts in our arms than the scrapes on
our knees.
This is the violence of learning
our time is here and

we

must

grow

up.

012. strange flaunt, but alas
/ pink

When she walks into the room,
we pretend not to know her.
Don't you remember the rules?
We treat her like slumber,
no one sees when we *enjoy* her.
The rules say that you are
"too much of a girl" if you wear her.
Coral and bubblegum are for the younger,
the older, not of the vibrant and of the lover.
The rules say if you *like* her you also like boys,
but not the right boys.
All the boys, the boys who sing
and the boys with side-swept hair,
the princes and the paupers fair.
If you are *her,*
you are pretty, not *smart.*
You are smiles and bubblegum *pops,*
crossed out with pens
and a room full of man's laughter.
Or is it the girls that are laughing?
I hear them gathered around the bathroom sinks,
and they say through diamond-lined teeth,
 "I hate the color pink."
But I've found, by the age of nineteen
that I love a coral colored bath and a blushing sky,
a raspberry morning and carnation afternoons,
lip-glossed evenings and lilac-smoked midnights.

When she walks into the room, I know her.
She is a bouquet of roses that were not sent to me
by a boy.
I bought them for myself, for my mother,
for the older and the younger and for the lover.
I love her even when she is blisters
and mosquito bites and sunburns.
God would not create a color
He meant for us to hate
or scorn
or attribute
to
girl.
It is strange,
the ways in which we flaunt.
But alas,
we are
girl.

013. I like your hair

"I like your hair," I say,
but what I really mean is,
"I like how your hair reminds
me of soft summer songs,
of strawberry milk
and clouds in my palms.
I think that, when it is summer,
your hair curls at the ends in sweat
and sticks to your blushed cheeks and neck.
I imagine you pushing your bangs from your brow
with the back of your hand
because the sun is laughing now.
Everything is laughing.
Mother.
Father.
Sister.
Friend.
Teacher.

Not you.

The list goes on in sickening charm.
The sun is still laughing
when you write those names down your arm.

I think your hair is like that of a fairy
because your blistered hands and bruised knees
do not speak of the war you carry
deep within the chasm of your body.

Slamming bedroom door,
boy's room, your clothes on his floor
        (not enough)
Slipping grades,
curses across your chest in bold red letters
        (not enough)
Cigarette poised between mouth and fingers
        (thought and choice)
        (dance and deed)
        NOT ENOUGH.

You look into the mirror and see a hurricane,
you see a body as a puddle after the rain.

So you dye your hair
because you want attention
without screaming so loud for it.
You want attention
because you find part of yourself broken."

I know this.
But I do not say this.
Instead, I set down your tray
and your cherry coke and say,
 "I like your hair."

014. sister

The boys make excuses to talk to my sister,
making their ways through glowing rooms
with diamond teeth and skin like moons.

It is origami, the way they pursue her.
For they fold themselves into a flower,
beg to be put in her window,
call her the sun,
the oxygen,
the water,
and she lets them.

Not months after, the boys are making excuses
for why they talk to my sister no longer.
"She isn't in my class anymore."
"She lives too far away."
"She's nine months older than me."
"I don't have a car, we can't go on dates."

My sister is fifteen,
going on sixteen,
innocent as a rose.
No, she is not only a rose
but the full garden,
glaring red and thorns and all.
She is all of it.
She is a full bouquet,
the vase in the window sill,
the whole window,

the whole room,
the whole house,
the sidewalk and the street.

And *you*,
the boy,
you are the cracks
and the potholes,
the oil spills and
the weeds in the driveways.

I do not wonder why you want her,
but why you do not,
and why she still does.

015. mornings, or maybe
I am mourning

I remember this house before you first moved in,
right after your parents bought it
and you had just received your first kitten.
He chased us across the empty, un-furnished floors
while we played a Selena Gomez CD
your brother had given you for Christmas.
And that night we laid together on the air mattress
and you snorted a pixie stick and asked for my
blessing.
You made me ache more than anyone,
I could not breathe, my ribs were too tight.
Because here, I see you in pastels,
in your grandmother's pond and trampoline,
when we walk to the store at the end of your street
and stretch out on the roof to dream.
That is where you took hours to eat your cookies n'
cream.
And now, in the mornings,
when the wrappers and cardboard boxes
and empty grape soda containers liter this same
floor,
now furnished and glowing in the morning light,
I scour your cupboards for pop tarts, and not
finding any,
I settle on another Rice Crispy Treat.
These mornings, I feel like we are strangers
who have spent these years walking beside each
other.

You see, I don't know your favorite songs anymore.
I don't know how many times your heart has been
broken.
I haven't seen you cry in years.
I've seen you laugh when you talk about yourself,
I see your eyes when I am telling my heart
and your own story blooms bright in your mind.
It is as if you forget I am there,
your own life is too beautiful and bright too care.
You have beautiful eyes and a beautiful mind.
I wish I knew it better than I do now.
It is morning, my friend,
or maybe I am mourning.

016. breakfast but slow

When the sky breaks its spine
to spill light into my window,
I feel the cracks in my mind and body
fill like they're laden with promise,
but really it's just strawberry milk
and later, I'll have a belly ache.

Stop.
We aren't thinking about later.

If I could stretch mornings
into days and bask in sunlight for weeks,
while I sip the milk at the bottom
of my cereal bowl,
maybe I would stop considering
all the ways I will batter my bones today.

Stop, you're thinking about later again.

Listen, though.
Later is bound to come,
let us be prepared for it.
So I put on my armor of brain cells,
and wish I had time to drink enough water,
but what is water compared to the blood
that will be spilled?

Wait.
Stop.
Later is for later.
Think about now.

So I shower.
And the water is warm,
my skin feels like something I'm meant to wear,
and there's not a part of me I want to scratch away.

Later, I will.
When the day truly starts,
when I start collecting the stares of others
like a bank of criteria I should write on my palms,
so everytime I use my hands,
I'll be reminded that someone somewhere
doesn't think I'm *good* enough.

The slow morning tells me to stop.
Tells me that someone somewhere didn't take their
morning slow enough.
They didn't stop to drink the milk at the bottom of
their cereal bowl,
they didn't run their fingers through the light on
their shower wall,
they didn't say good morning to their mother.

They fled through the first hours,
ignoring the sky,
and collecting stares,
collecting failures before they're ever even made.

So the morning tells me,
"Take me slow. Sip me like hot coffee.
Live in me as much as you feign to
live the rest of your day, and perhaps
your day won't feel like reeling from string
to a perilous ground.
Let the sky break it's spine,
Don't break your own."

017. mango street

The pink-tiled bathrooms and velvet robes have
been traded in for patched-up aprons and
flour-dusted hands.

Where names were once stitched into lilac silk,
the phases of the moon are inked across
collar-bones.

The wives drink wine from mason jars,
and prune their ferns and poplars.

The children sing to the sidewalk songs of plagues,
and they think not of fevers but of their mother's
gardens.

The fences are white and the houses yellow, and if
you listen you can hear the *thunk* of a knife against
a cutting board.

The tea goes cold on cracked counters, but what is
colder, and more worn are the soles of their feet

which tread hard-wood floors and gardens
everyday.
The hands are tired, the faces like bent cardboard.

They have not forgotten their so-called golden days,
you should not think that because of their now
dimmed ways.

For when they look at the kitchen sink at night, they see glitter and smoke and homemade dynamite.

During the day, they just nod and tell their children that the chalk on the pavement depicts something *interesting*.

Still, living is still a thread in the aprons. It is hot showers and the sun through the boughs of the orange trees.

It is the chalk on the pavement and the children falling over in a circle.

For, you see, one day the party girls grew up, and they moved to Mango Street.

018. the burning days

These are the days of raspberry whispers
and magnolia kisses on sunburned cheeks.
A tender riot shakes these streets,
these quiet, quaking trees.
I have felt every morning break in two,
a riot of color and the succumb of the sidewalk.
This interlude splinters, leaving shards in my
palms.
A newborn star is curled on my tongue, bracing on
the roof of my mouth.
The colors are kind to him, I say.
Kinder than they ever are to me.
He is boy: friend of colors.
Like gold and blood red.
Boy smokes dandelions in summers arms, sucks
dreams from her breasts,
turns those dreams into butterflies,
A butterfly in his palm, closing a fist around it.

019. the blue gabled house

The blue gabled house is a page splattered in paint. Smiles are yellow, and tears are teal smudged with gray, cardboard faces crinkle in concentration, flesh wrinkles in worriment. It sees eyes glistening with joy, mangled souls on the verge of healing on a window sill. Or breaking on the lip of a bathtub. The house likes to stretch the thin, shimmering bond of humans in the light of morning. It catches a wisp of a promise, glimmering gold. It drops it into a glass of milk and gulps it down with a bubbling laugh.

020. natural disaster

There are thunderstorms inside of me.
Hurricanes inside of me.
Earthquakes inside of me.
Wildfires inside of me.
There are days when I feel like a natural disaster.
This is hunger and thirst and frustration,
not for food and water and recognition,
but to feel like I am valued when I am not *making
something*.
Becoming something.
It is okay to be still, I need to say.
To sing.
To live.
I need to rest.
God, I need to rest.

021. (un)becoming

I am becoming okay with knowing
that there is always more becoming.
We speak and write and sing of all the ways
we can be better, kinder, more loving,
more beautiful and admired.
We make conversation with ourselves
about *becoming*,
but we often forget that there is also an
unbecoming.
For there is a breaking
& a reckoning
& an ultimatum.
One day, you will die.
What will you become then?

022. *bandaids and aspirin*

A ground of ice, air of the sun,
its tongue slipping around me,
and I am swallowed by morning,
as I finish digesting the night.

Salt on my tongue,
sugar slipping through my fingers,
I walk through darkness,
but I can see light through the cracks
in the forest.

The earth bends it spine,
allows my feet to sink into its skin.
If I take my own crown off my heart
and let it beat, open,
free, held in the hands of heaven.

In this safety, I can collapse, my limbs
knocking together.
Run, legs bound in my own bandages.
When I am here,
I am not collecting stares,
not counting judgments,
or other's perceptions.

This here, is my mind when I am healing.

This is how I heal,
soaking in an hour in what
feels like a stretch of time between
the first beating of my heart
to when I reach heaven,
This is the aspirin.
And the water, finding myself
under it, allowing my wounds to stain it,
are the bandaids.

Because wearing the bandaids
and taking the aspirin
is my way of apologizing to myself,
Of saying, "I'm sorry for doing all
those things that made you unlike
yourself," so maybe, possibly,
the stares would turn to other sorts of
looks like smiles, and approving nods,
and eyes lifting in pride.

023. *after the party*

the silence deepens like my mother's hand
does in the dough and it rests.
The stillness of the morning
midst the clutter makes us one.
The house and me.
I am the floorboards and the wallpaper.
I am the creaks and groans.
The house is breathing
as we pick up broken plates
and shattered glasses.
It is wearing the golden streamers like ribbons
and the glitter on the floor as eyeshadow.
A soft, shaky laugh brushes the halls.
The walls, *I* shudder.
And smile.

024. ode to the 12 years of my formal education

The cytoplasm refers to all of the cellular material inside the plasma membrane, other than the nucleus. You can find the rate at which a block is going to slide down an incline at a velocity of 2.3 meters per second using Newton's second law of motion. And I'm supposed to know the square root of 231, but instead I am asking how this will help in the real world, as if what I'm learning cannot be defined as real if it is also hard. I would ask, how does knowing the square root of 231 help in real, hard times?

Because what if like the zombie apocalypse, or like alien invasion, our world brinking on eternal eclipse, or like Jesus is coming back and evil is rearing its horns, eyes reddened and what if we're the next Christians to be beheaded?

I would rather know how to kneel for my Savior in heaven, than to kneel for a vessel of evil even while he is still human. So now, knowing the square root of 231 doesn't seem as important. But since I love the Lord, I want to know the square root of 231 because it is part of the language with which He built this world.

And the cytoplasm of a cell is only a shred of reason to prove why He is Lord. Learning doesn't end when I get a job, it's like why would I ever want my love for God to end so why would I want my love for learning to end?

So if you want a job working for another man rather than working for the Lord, find yourself a test written by man for man rather than opening the word of God and living, because living, living and learning is the true test and praying is the preparation.

I would rather be up until 4 in the morning on my knees praying than finding that I'm drowning, drowning in sums that seem like they'll never amount to anything.

You see, the destination is not another institution of education built by men with misperceptions that this world is all that there is but the destination is home with our Lord.

So while I do know what a cytoplasm is, how to find velocity, what the square root of 231 is, I also know how to lead, how a conversation can change the course of a life, how to find inspiration in even the dullest of stories.

And my love of the Lord is reflected in quoting Atticus Finch, in my words which I craft in an effort to be like Bronte and Dickens. I've found that the words of Christ far outweigh those of Aristotle, Homer, and Darwin. Which means his words can outweigh the great thinkers of today.

You see leaning on the Lord rather than leaning on a grade means I'm learning of God, I'm knowing the lord, and I do not need to know the world. The world does not need to know me.

And by the way,
the square root of 231 is 15.1986841536

025. don't take it personally

Don't take it personally
but when told to sit back down
and stay pretty,
I think of standing up in a crowded church,
sending the organ into flames,
and asking all to bow to her majesty,
for she enters, diamond on her teeth,
moons on her cheeks,
and hurricanes beneath her eyes.
You would call yourselves wise
but when wise is *teenage girl*
it is the slaughter of "likes" and question marks
in the pulpit that is inevitable to rise.
It is pretty lies and pretty whys,
for we all like to look at pretty things
but no one wants to *be* a pretty thing.
Not anymore, for it is dangerous.
No one goes window shopping anymore.
They break in and steal and then they shatter
on the sidewalk, crush what they've stolen
beneath their boots and shiny new cars.
Others might see it in broad daylight
but they will turn the other way.
Where have the shopkeepers gone?
Where have the police gone?
Where have the *fathers* gone?
No one hears my questions.
So when I commit arson in this fashion
and you call it "breaking the law" for attention,

I will remember that you are but a moth
crushed in your own clay house.
This is the same as before -
ramah and sodom and gomorrah.
But please,
don't take it personally.

026. the blue gabled house II

The blue gabled house has seen everything, *it thinks.*
Until today.

A mangled soul drops itself on the porch, and inserts a brass key into the lock. It steps into a cheery hall shadowed by the setting sun.

The house stills, snaps into silence.

Its smile fades, and it grows curious. It holds its breath,
the promise of a crescendo is broken by the dull *thud* of the soul dropping its suitcase to the wood floors.

The house turns to peer at the mangled form, and finds that the boy, well, *his body is a museum.*

His body is a museum, because there is history in every bend of his joints. Or perhaps he is a cardboard home barely holding itself together.

On his hands, the house can see the years spent bent over a piano where the keys are his dreams he shatters because his fingers land too hard on the flats and sharps.

His back still aches from the memory, and in his feet, the floorboards of the house finds the years he's spent trying to tread down his demons in ballet shoes.

He rises on the tips of his toes, pure strength in his legs because he can hold himself up like this, when there is music in his veins and sound in his mind.

But right now, as he turns to look at his new home, he feels the walls clattering around him. The blue-gabled house knows that he is finding the cracks in the walls, the dents in the floors.

And it shifts to let in the light of a June evening where the sun is leeking itself through the windows like the last drops of wine at the lip of the bottle.

And the light looks sweet, it falls over a piano that is battered and bruised by the twins that use to live here.

The house blows a breath, sending dust shifting across the floors so that the mangled can see that there is history here too.

History because this place has been a home to many who've dropped themselves like broken china on its doorstep.

The house smiles, lays a hand on his shoulder, and whispers, "The kitchen is around the corner, and it knows how to heal quite well."

The blue gabled house says, "Welcome home. You don't have to be broken here. You can be many pieces, and I can be the string. Because here...the pasts of others stain the walls, and you are not alone."

027. my body as a home

This is making my own body my home:
by remembering all my previous joys
and how to trust and hold myself
in the dark as well as the light.
It is talking to a stranger who is screaming
and remembering that this isn't personal
unless I take it so.

It is learning to smile
at myself
and not
just others.

It is responsibility.
It is spring cleaning in mind,
clearing out aches in my bones,
unfluring failures gathered in my ribs.

028. another body as a home

There is a part of me that wants a wall in my house
where I can write every place I have seen a sunset
until there are exactly a hundred of them.

From a back porch over a cricket-buzzed field.
From a rooftop in New York City.
From a cliffedge somewhere warm and stormy.

But there is another part of me that wants to see
your eyes a hundred times when we look at a
sunset.
I want to remember every place you've held my
hand and told me that this is what love feels like:
going everywhere but never feeling like you left
home.

029. am I fortune's fool?
and other musings

There was a boy who loved me but not enough.
He made himself the muse,
bent himself over a piano,
plucked his heart out, made it black and white.
He wonders if he has run out of luck,
if the universe has tricked him,
if this is surely the lot that God has cast for him.
The fortunate know how to kiss pretty girls,
he only knows how to make songs about them.

I like to romanticize being misunderstood.
I think he does too.
I think that is why I could never love him,
because I found something in him
that I loved too much about myself.
I see now that it was not loving myself,
it was not loving myself well at all.
For I cannot love myself if I do not tell myself the
truth.

030. *what would the walls say?*

What would the walls say
if they had tongues like we do,
guns in their mouths,
and bullets in their paraphrasing.

They would tell the tale
of a boy as a torn veil,
torn between sacrament
and sacrifice,
stained glass and rose edifice.

The cherry stain of twilight
on the torn wallpaper
hails june - advent of summer
and of you.

I fear that one day summer will end
and it will not feel like this;
like a tender ache as sweet
as the raspberry-kissed sky.

We trip over rainbows
winding down through this land once divine,
this forsaken elysium
ruptured eden, broken rind,
this tarnished rye.

You are summer:
fleeting, tender and aching
and always returning.
It is you and all this undoing.

031. *he tells me his secrets over tea*

He drinks tea.
His mother knows that he drinks tea,
for she has learned his secrets as I have:
in watching his gaze avert,
in the rise and fall of his chest as he sleeps,
the degree of tightness in his embrace,
in how he greets a Sunday morning
and spends her afternoon.
she knows, *I* know
because I spill my secrets in the same way.
I drink tea—but only a few sips.
I don't like it cold.
I don't hold his gaze for long,
my eyes look for roses and torn corners instead.
I sleep on my side,
my hand holding my lower stomach when I bleed.
I embrace a Sunday morning like a favorite aunt
coming for a visit.
but by afternoon she is an overgrown garden,
an empty chair still rocking in the corner.
one day I will be the mother:
the tea is cold and untouched.
There is no time to drink tea.
my eyes will be everywhere at once.
I will still sleep on my side,
on the edge of a precipice.
the blankets are ice
so I hold everything in a tight embrace.
Sunday mornings are answered prayers,

my chest eases, burdens lifted.
Her afternoons are my muse.
his question hangs above his teacup,
it follows me through the evening until my cheek is numb on the countertop.
"darling, how many metaphors will you use to hide your secrets?"
He knows that I keep metaphors like knives in a drawer.
his mother does.
a gun beneath my mattress.
his mother does.
mace behind the mirror in the front hall.
his mother does.
He knows I speak defense and sing bullets.
his mother does.
but he is not afraid.
he is a whetstone,
the key to the drawer,
the bed frame firm,
the moonlight reflecting in the mirror.
He is safe.
he pours me a hot cup of tea.
my fingers trace the rim,
I pretend it is his mouth.
I tell him his secrets,
and he tells me mine.
I drink the whole cup of tea.
It does not go cold.

032. boy as a poppy field

my brother told me that you vape on your breaks.
my friend told me that you like older girls
because, to you, it's a higher stake.

they say your choice in friends isn't *smart*
because they make sport of hurling "slut."

they say that one time you made out with the girl
your best friend liked *right in front of him.*

they say this is the second time you have cut that
best friend out of your life.

you say you have changed homes,
changed jobs,
changed schools
in a handful of simmering months.
These choices blister your palms.

I do not respond with much,
because what I would say of you can not be spoken
with
"I heard"
or,
"I saw"
or, "They tell me that…"

because you are a field of poppies,
red and blooming and suffocating.
I would lie down within you and forget my mind.
I would have visions and dreams and then nothing.

You hand yourself around in pieces
to girls with soft smiles and confidence in their
futures.
You contemplate the universe,
you know it's meaning and God.

But you don't know where to take yourself.
Home?
You go to a friend's house and you pretend to love
and care.
But your heart only knows to stare
from afar.

033. I ask him what he believes

and I want him to tell me a
truth that doesn't seek to cleave
my mortal flesh into hundreds of misdeeds.
I want his mouth to be an echo of a prayer
he prayed when he was young
that he would know love
as a rose garden without the thorns,
a fountain without the cracks worn
and coppery taste of wishes wasted.

While you sell absolutions
on a corner of conviction and condemnation,
I fear most that it is only from afar you will see
heaven.

I knew this would hurt the moment
I saw Mary hanging from your neck.
Still, I ventured through,
cutting myself on stained glass
and choking on holy water.
I am *drunk* on holy water.
Is that blasphemy?
Is it blasphemy that you will not know the love
of someone who knows that they are good enough
while you spend your life folded into shadow
telling every confessor that they are not good
enough?

So call me the thief on the cross beside yours,
the one who sought to steal your heart
but was caught red-handed and blistered.
Still, I hang,
with the nails of your absolution in my palms.
Is it blasphemy, that I would summon storms to
tear your life-long woven tapestry
down the center and raise armies to fight for you?

When you were born,
 they sprinkled you with religion
 like you were to be a garden
 except the seeds grew guilt.
The roses around your wrists
match the scars on mine.

034. tinder

You asked me if I would hate you if you had tattoos or long hair or a nice car, and I tell you I stay because you love me in a white dress, not the black one, and because you are a whole night sky in brown eyes and hands the size of mine - striking and full of wonder. You are lightning and thunder but afraid of storms. But you love the rain, we both love the rain, and feeling sane, passing between us anxiety and dreams and pain.

I stay because you let me see you cry and you call me at 3 a.m. because as I have slept these past 3 hours you have done just that: cried.

I stay because when you told me that pineapple doesn't belong on pizza and I replied with "K," you didn't leave me.

And after thirty plus stitches and the surgeon's news was that you might lose your pinkie, you thought I would leave you.

But I would stay if you lost five fingers, ten fingers, a whole hand, a whole arm. You are more than a limb, and I would rather lose every one of my own limbs before I lose you.

So now, I thank you for swiping right and messaging first and meeting me at IHOP at 11 p.m.

even though you didn't know if I really existed.
I thank you for reading my books and going to church.

And I promise that when we play Foosball and I *win*, I will not blame it on your absent limb.

Too soon?
Probably.
And for that, I am sorry.

But I am not sorry for all the sunset pictures I've texted you and poems and rants about the public education system.

I am not sorry
or regretful
or ashamed
of you
or your body
or Tinder.

035. he says sorry for not kissing me while we
are standing outside of a waffle house

(now)

The turn at the bottom of the hill
feels like *almost home*,
because in the matter of a minute
I'll be in his arms.
I can count the seconds.
For there are no traffic lights
or stop signs on the way up.
Just one, busy winding road,
his smile and arms at the end.

(rewind to before)

We sat in his car for three to four hours
and I told him everything I've ever wanted
to tell someone but was too afraid to say.
I said them because if he ran away then,
I wouldn't be all that hurt and it would feel like
the discomfort of a limb losing circulation
or a blister on my heal.
It was dusk when he leaned against his car door
and asked me what color my eyes were.
I told him blue but what I meant was,
whatever the color of hope is,
and I hope that is what he sees.

(the close)

I wish I could write poems
about every part of him.
(his laugh and smile,
the calm of his and the wild.)
But you see, he is already
a poem himself, pouring into me,
So, you see, it is hard to write
poetry about a poem that already is.
So I will write about
how I feel instead.

    It is this way because he is kind,
    because he says sorry for not
    kissing me while we are
    standing in front of a waffle house.
    and I do not need him to say
    that he is sorry, but I like when he
    does.

You see, there was this one day where
we drove through the hills of northern
kentucky where it is okay to be free
and no one is watching *(not really)*
when you roll down the windows while
it is raining and sing.

    Here, with him, there is everything,
    And I do not need to be
    anything beyond myself.

He does not need to be anything
but the poetry he already is.

036. *how to stay a child*

I ask him what he believes
and what I really want to know
is not what he believes now but
what he believed when he was a child.

Because once upon a time,
we all believed in such things
as our parents and grandparents living forever,
and always, always staying young while we grow.

I wish I still knew how to be a child.
for within every dream of mine,
there is a child who only wants to
trace their fingertips across
the surfaces that have known thousands of
strangers
and shift colors in and out of tear-blurred focus.
There are too many stars to count,
to many winds to feel,
and colors to create to not stay a child
even at nineteen,
and twenty,
and every year after.

I do not need a camera to remember,
only a poet's vocabulary and a child's memory.

037. the absence of stars

Missing him is like the absence of stars,
it is a sunburn on an overcast day.
It is knowing that some things that die
are most beautiful before they do.

It is being kissed with a quiet hunger.
It is savoring, not devouring the way
he satiates such a feeling,
for he does it for me as much as for him.

038. aestatis amorum

Summer is for falling in love
with calamine colored skies
and lilac bruised pavements
and you in the front seat of your car.
I fall in love best when it is summer.
I can love the color of a sunburn or blister
as well as the blinking restaurant lights
deep into the August night.
Risks are worth taking when the air smells
like promises and everything is alive
and consequences are for turning into poems.

039. this is the ultimatum

I cannot love you (him)
if you (he) cannot love
the One who made me.

040.

Saffira turned and said,
"One day, I hope to tell you everything, Riah,
And that it will break you."

-   *Court of Curses*

041. February 11th

On February 11th, 2020
I told you that I loved you.
It was 3 a.m. or around that time
and I had driven to your house
in the middle of the night to tell
you something bigger than
"I want you" or "I can wait for you,"
and all the way there I prayed for
courage that I would leave this
behind if I needed to.
But He tells me to stay
because all those years I asked for one
boy and then the other He was saying,
"I have something better."
And when you told me you loved me back
I did not believe you,
not until I told you my fears about people
only caring about me *(reading my books)*
when I became famous,
and successful,
was *making money*.
You cried and cried and cried
and held and held and held me.
I believed, then, that you loved me.
That was the first time I could whisper
your name in the dark and it felt like
everything.

042. after solomon

This is what the end of a season feels like:
like I am a silver cord severed,
a golden bowl broken,
a pitcher shattered at the fountain,
a wheel fractured at the cistern.

There are mourners in the streets.
The mourners are my dreams
limping by because they have forgotten
how to remember in their youth,
how to stay children when they are grown.

043. the ache of august II

When I speak of the boys I have loved who were born in August,

I do not mean I fell in love with boys who were born in August.

And by this I mean I fell in love with them in my mind, but not in theirs.

I fell in love with fields at dusk and blackberry patches,

the stain of such a fruit on their lips and calloused fingertips.

August is for dreaming, birthdays are for remembering.

Boys in blackberry patches at dusk are for pretending

we have futures that are not ours and one day, when I love a boy

who's birthday may not be in august, we might pick blackberries at dusk,

and it will not be pretend.

044. the knife drawer

So I sigh, the sound seeming
to pull everything from me.
I tell him that I am running
out of metaphors.
He smiles, it looks like knives.
"Darling, you are the metaphor."

> This is what it is,
> when I let Satan sing songs
> to me in the deep of night.

045. saving yourself

Salvation is not a sold-out show.
Salvation is not a *show*.
One cannot walk in and sit in cushioned seats.
There are no curtains to be drawn,
for the curtain was split down the center
that morn when the storms were like trickling
streams compared to the cries of thieves
and of the Advocate nailed to trees.
Salvation is not a ticket,
(but if it were it'd be one way)
It is not a stub, not a prize we pocket
by spilling sliver.
It is a gift.
And a choice.
You can return it if you wish.
There are days when I would rather
thirty pieces of silver gather
in these pockets,
only to find that God put holes in those pockets.
There is a note stitched on the inside,
saying that one day wrath will stir itself into
eternity
and salvation will close its doors.
Forever.

046. a Savior's pursuit

you traverse this grim grandeur as if it were your
home,
because where we see the rubble and ruin of a
reckless rebellion,
of a fragile feeling pinched between trembling
fingers,
you see confetti and smoke,
the screams of thousands
basking in the same feeling,
the same revolution.
Where we hear curses thrown back and forth
between two players from a window four stories up,
You hear a symphony
a drum beat—a calling.
We're the confetti,
You are the eager hands reaching.
You would pour your blood onto the rubble
to make it shine.
These rundowns of legends become castle grounds,
the sagging fences
gates of pearls.
You would call us saints
when we feel like mere soldiers
"You don't have to fight anymore...
I already fought for you...
The dragon beneath your bed is slain,
the monsters punching through the calm of your
head are but mere decay."
We see a desert,

You see a street paved in forgotten good intentions,
in forgiveness.
Grim is such a curse,
a door we open each hour to beckon in a new
horror,
because what is flesh but fleeting wind?

"Now as the king of Israel was passing by on the wall, a woman cried out to him, saying, 'Help, my lord, O king!'

And he said, 'If the Lord will not help you, how shall I help you? From the threshing floor, or from the winepress?' And the king asked her, 'What is your trouble?'

She answered, 'This woman said to me, "Give your son, that we may eat him today, and we will eat my son tomorrow." So we boiled my son and ate him. And on the next day I said to her, "Give your son, that we may eat him." But she has hidden her son'"

2 Kings 6:26-29

047. ramah

Two eyes plucked,
two pillars plunder,
this is a song we sing in thunder.
A prophet in a well,
a king in a cell,
this is a song we sing of Hell.
A prophet mute,
a prophet and a prostitute.
All through the night
the wailing breaks this city's blight.
The mothers...
they have eaten their children.

048. judgement day I

I know the venom of a lamb slaughtered
at the edge of the road.
The door of the house beyond drips with its blood
as if the man beyond is so desperate for salvation
he thinks that the only way to obtain it is by
absolution.

So he calls slaughter purgation and
the destruction of love blossomed
in the hollow of late summer a sacrament.
He baptizes himself in poison,
and the cure is beyond his reach.

049. judgment day II

I watch the end of the world from an apple tree,
its boughs are bent in the wind,
but the leaves are not screaming and wailing as the
ground does.
It is breathing sweet songs,
and the horizon is bleeding.
But in the arms of this tree
I see the bruised purple of the sky above
and the flood waters rising.
There is no ark to save me,
no dove to find an island.
There is only heaven awaiting me.
So I close my eyes and let the world end upon me.

050. pious collision II

Thomas doubted and Peter denied,
Judas kissed and Jesus died.
I wake up and check my phone,
I collect stares in my palms
and stitch into me failures before they're made.
I somehow doubt that God will hold me when I toss
into bed
my battered bones, bruised ego and everything
that's bled.
I deny that my own strength will one day break
beneath these ill-triumphs and the flaming stake.
I kiss a boy thinking he will wrap my wounds
in wine instead of vinegar,
that he will kiss me back with honey instead of
hyssop.
I forget that Jesus died
so I could live.
He died so that doubt and denial would drown
and I would not kiss just to feel myself
as a crumbling wall, each piece peeling into a moat
of my own bloodstreams and slaughtered hope.
He died so that I could kiss Him on the cheek
and not be rewarded with silver sleek
and a rope around my neck for forever sleep.

051. *sometimes, I am Judas*

In the morning, I kiss Jesus on the
cheek.
I am running, and over my shoulder
I am shouting,

"I love you!"
But words like

"Later"
and,

"After"
and,

"Maybe"
are somehow stronger.

They are nails in His palms,
and my flesh is the hammer.

052. ...and then, love

In songs and in poems
people tend to speak of love
as something only found in the forms
of hurricanes and oceans,
a breaking mountain,
a split chasm.
But I've found it in the floorboards
when the morning light leaks
through my bent bones
and spills like gold over my fingers.
I drink orange juice and take hot showers,
and I know that love is not a natural disaster
but a natural birthright.
As if we ever had "rights" to begin with.

053. after tyler joseph

This is poetry: the way we love,
the way we pursue things that are fleeting
yet promise to return, like seasons,
and inspiration and ambitions.
It is confetti on the floor after all the fans have left.
It is the quiet after all has been loaded back into the
buses.
It is a stage bathed in green and yellow light but
empty.
It is standing in an arena and seeing all your ghosts
in the seats.
They are not clapping or cheering.
They are sleeping because you haven't written a
new song in months.
You sing the same songs and we all cry.
We cry and cry and cry.
Tonight - ten thousand people will keep their lives
because you asked them to stay alive.
So in this quiet after the show,
you ask yourself, "Why am I alive?"
It is this.
All of this.
Do not look at all the confetti that has been left
behind.
There is more in the pockets of those who left.
Their hands warm, hearts warmer.

I write poems at Twenty One Pilots concerts

054. how I'm getting over it

Moving on is taking everything
that once felt right,
clenching them in your fists
and standing on a cliff-edge.
Below, there is water.
Above, there is a storm.
Moving on is standing on the edge and not
throwing everything that once
felt right into the water.
It is swallowing it whole,
downing it with an ocean.
It is bitter what was once sweet.
It is swallowing your pride
and leaving it behind.

055. the answer to the first problem

A long time ago, before a thirty-three year old
carpenter died nailed to a tree and saved the world,

there was the wisest king in the world who said,
"Behold, you are beautiful, my love;
Behold, you are beautiful;
your eyes are doves."

And long before the wisest king in the world died,
his kingdom split in two,
there was a man who gave up his hair, his eyes, his
strength, his life, for love.

And long before this man killed one-thousand of his
captors while blind,
there was a garden given to a man to learn to love
before he was given woman,

for God said, *"It is not good for man to be alone."*

056. this is woman

There are some stories we leave behind,
between the pages and the lines
of condemnation and conviction.

> It is Hagar and Tamar,
> Shimera and Puna,
> Rebekah and Leah,
> Rahab and Ruth,
> Delilah and Dinah,
> Deborah and Jael,
> Hilduah and Miriam,
> Abigail and Bathsheba,
> Esther and Sheba,
> Lydia and Priscilla
> and Phoebe.

It is the concubine of a Levite
who was gangraped and killed
by Benjamites and cut into pieces
to be sent throughout all of Israel.

> It is the woman who dropped
> an upper millstone on
> Abimelech's head
> who said before it could kill
> him, "Draw your sword and
> kill me, lest men say of me,
> *'A woman killed him.'* "

This is how it begins:
with a womb and a tree
that is as tantalizing
as oozing mangos on a
blistering, ninety-degree day.
It is summer swollen,
and it is Eve not knowing
what she does not know.

It is Mary in the supermarket,
buying produce for soup to
feed the twelve men at her
house who sit and wait and
mourn their teacher.
They sit and wait and mourn,
but she was the one
who buried Him in the tomb.

057. write your dreams down

A small house with many windows.
A small kitchen with something yellow.
Painting every morning and writing every night.
On our street grows fruits: mangos, oranges,
tangerines and lemons.
We are mother and father to an Australian
Shepherd.
Scotland, Italy, Thailand, Israel, New York, Hawaii.
Treehouses and bananas.
Wearing nothing but bikinis and oversized t shirts.
Barefoot all the time.
Room for all my books and room for all the books
yet to come.
Reading to my children once they have come.
Having room for my children to have room for
books when they come.
Bike rides.
Eating strawberries every morning.
Running around in fields on overcast days.
2 a.m. runs to Waffle House.
My mother not being worried when I am not home
at 2 a.m.
Dancing to a Lorde song at my wedding.
'...I'm on fire, but when we're dancing it's alright'
Befriending children and elephants and old men
who sit alone in restaurants.
Collecting stories from strangers.
Memorizing constellations.
Learning a song well on the piano.

Becoming good at math so I can write that one book about a magician who uses physics to create all his tricks.
Reading every Shakespeare play.
Card games, cabin days, and midnight swims in the lake.
Heaven.

058. gluten free Jesus

A girl I worked with in a fast food joint
once told me a story about when she was
in catholic private school and her religion
teacher told her that communion was the
reincarnated blood and body of Jesus Christ.
She raised her hand, a dare, and asked for the truth.
What if you have a gluten allergy?
How do you make Jesus gluten free?

And this is how it goes:
The religion teacher sends her to the principal,
gives her detention, does not call on her when her
hand is raised high.

This is what we do:
We ask questions and do not expect honest
answers.
We are asked questions and we do not give honest
answers.

This is what we like to remember:
That God and being saved and everything made is
for us to define.

What we forget:
Is that a thirty-three year old carpenter was
whipped thirty-nine times, given vinegar to drink,
and nailed on a cross for six hours before He died.
We do not ask Him how it felt to die.

We ask how we can make Him exactly how we want Him to be.

059. tayler.

She is lying on the sidewalk
counting her own freckles
and breaking her barbie's arms,
and I am tracing her with chalk.
I am dusting blue her knees and the bends
of her elbows and dips of her dimples
and adoring how when she laughs
her eyes close all the way
and her cheeks bloom red
like balloons or roses or apples.
We meet at age five
and then there begins the demise
of my vibrancy, my transparency, my pliancy.
Beside her I am muted, I am diluted.
Everything I am becomes a response to her,
a reaction, a thread pulled taut that she will break
with a laugh or a joke or flirtation.
She is wild and doesn't care what anyone thinks
but at the same time, she cares what I think.
She doesn't think she doesn't do, she sings.
She sings on my front porch until I finish
my dinner and emerge into the summer dusk.
We play mothers and singers
and we forget that we are children
and that it is better that we do not know
how to hurt each other.
She moves in November
and I am ten or eleven and have yet to remember,
that she will move to Indiana

and in a few years from now,
it won't even matter
all the songs we have written together.
But I am nineteen now and so is she,
And I hope she is still singing.

060. nineteen

(this is a journal entry written on January 22nd, 2020)

I am trying to make a habit out of journaling more often because I know it heals and because one day, I will be able to look back on it and remember.

I have been discontent, frustrated, and anxious since November, I would say. It was not bad at first, but it has been getting worse. Most nights I fall asleep anxious. I am not paranoid about sleep or failures the next day as what made me anxious during highschool. Rather, I am just anxious.

I think, sometimes, that I feel this way because I have a tendency to romanticize not being "okay" as if there is one solid definition of what "okay" is. In many ways, I am quite okay. I have a steady stream of income, a comfortable bed to sleep in every night, food in my stomach when I fall asleep, people who love and care for me and I get to write every day. In fact, I am much more than just okay. But yet, I am still anxious.

I am struggling with this transitionary period of my life a lot more than I thought I would. I welcomed (and still do) the uncertainty of writing for a living so that I would be forced to depend on God's plan for me (which is far better than my own). He has shown me every step of the way and I believe He will continue to do so.

Still, everyday I struggle with this impulse, this desire and frustration and yearning for something to shift and change. I want to pack necessities and a few prized possessions and go rogue in another country. I want to move out and into my own place where I can paint a wall dark teal and make it a gallery wall. I want to have lots of bookshelf space and a place to cook meals for myself every night. I want to toss myself onto my own couch in the evening and stare up at the ceiling and feel accomplished with the day. I want to quit my job suddenly and without remorse. But here is where I am ruled by fear and this notion that perhaps I desire all of this for attention and to make an impression.

I do not want to make decisions for the mere romanticism of it. I want to make them because the eternal effect will be...well, *good*. "And God said that it was very good," when He made male and female. I want this principle to be enamated into every facet of my life.

This is the struggle of an anxious, lonely yet not alone, 19-year-old sitting on the floor of her hallway. She wants to write and eat mangos without having a severe allergic reaction. She can only control one of these things. So she will write.

She will write and do the small impulsive things until she can do the big impulsive things. She will take long drives at night with the windows down and sing every Lorde song. She will download Tinder (or rather, she already did and hopes she will not feel inclined to do so again). She will smile at strangers and cut her hair short. She will try painting and start putting together that gallery wall she wants.

She will remember that these impulsive yearnings to travel and move out are better with people she loves - who love her- with her.

Love has saved her. It will always save her.

061. find someone

Find someone brave enough
to love you from across the room,
not just while you are in their arms
or looking into their eyes.

Find someone brave enough to say,
"I was hoping you could fix me,
but I realize that I have to do that myself."

062. hindsight

I once read somewhere that
the loss of innocence
begins when you realize
your parents are not perfect

and this is followed by
realizing that most boys
are not kind and most
girls are too resigned
to eating breadcrumbs
and calling themselves full.

Every summer, I nearly settle
for less and less.
Sometimes "less" is a boy
who does not know himself.
Sometimes "less" are the girls
with knives for tongues I get ice cream with.
Most times "less" are my expectations
which is why I find myself
nursing new and old wounds on
midsummer evenings as I sit barefoot
on my porch wishing I was in a field
somewhere far away in an apple tree
counting the stars as they appear.

In hindsight, everything hurts
and everything heals.
It takes mere seconds and heated,
rushing veins to hurt.
To damage and rupture and break.
It takes practice and patience to heal.

In hindsight,
I've never been lashed thirty-nine times
or been nailed to a tree for six hours.
I have never had to drink straight vinegar
or bleed from every part of my body.
I have never slept for three days inside a tomb,
I have never wandered a desert for forty days
without food or water.

In hindsight, this is nineteen -
aching and simmering
between the sendoff of eighteen
and the great welcome of becoming
something beyond *child*.

This is the ache to explore the world,
buy a tiny apartment and fill it with books,
all the while remembering that a girl
died at the age of nineteen burned alive.

Burn with the fever of creating,
& remembering,
& holding onto everything
that has kept you alive.

There are some things I will always have;
like healing and being saved.

Thank you:

To my mom for being my best teacher and for being strong even when you feel weak.

To my closest friends who hear me and hold me: Emma, Leah, Faith, and Lydia.

To my brother and sisters for making me laugh.

To Hunter for making me laugh and for holding me and letting talk about this thing called anxiety.

To Jesus who saved me.

To every anxious, lonely-yet-not-alone person who might read this. Thank you for existing.

Made in the USA
Columbia, SC
08 March 2020